★ **GREAT SPORTS TEAMS** ★

THE CHICAGO

BEARS

FOOTBALL TEAM

Tim O'Shei

Enslow Publishers, Inc.

40 Industrial Road   PO Box 38
Box 398   Aldershot
Berkeley Heights, NJ 07922   Hants GU12 6BP
USA   UK

http://www.enslow.com

To Ryan Johnsen, for your hard work and wonderful help.

Library of Congress Cataloging-in-Publication Data

O'Shei, Tim.
    The Chicago Bears football team / Tim O'Shei.
        p. cm. — (Great sports teams)
    Includes bibliographical references (p.) and index.
    ISBN 0-7660-1285-9
    1. Chicago Bears (Football team)—Juvenile literature. [1. Chicago Bears
(Football team). 2. Football—History.] I. Title. II. Series.
GV956.C5 O84   2001
796.332'64'0977311—dc21

                                                      00-012215

Printed in the United States of America

10 9 8 7 6 5 4 3 2 1

To Our Readers: We have done our best to make sure all Internet addresses in this
book were active and appropriate when we went to press. However, the author
and the publisher have no control over and assume no liability for the material
available on those Internet sites or on other Web sites they may link to. Any
comments or suggestions can be sent by e-mail to comments@enslow.com or to
the address on the back cover.

Illustration Credits: AP/Wide World Photos.

Cover Illustration: AP/Wide World Photos.

Cover Description: Walter Payton.

CONTENTS

*C*hicago Bears quarterback Jim McMahon roars out commands to his teammates during Super Bowl XX on January 26, 1986.

A SUPER WIN

At first glance, the 1985 Chicago Bears could be confused with a rock band: At center stage was Jim McMahon, lead singer, in headband and sunglasses. Rumbling behind was William "Refrigerator" Perry, a kitchen-sized man. Breaking smooth moves was Walter Payton, blessed with a high-pitched voice and the nickname Sweetness. Pacing along the side stage was tough-talking Mike Ditka, with blow-dried hair and a snarl that could scare even a bear.

Despite their rock 'n' roll appearance, this was a football club determined to accomplish what no Bears team had done for more than twenty years: win a championship.

A Super Goal

"You're only as good as your last game," Head Coach Ditka had told his team in training camp, "And our last game wasn't very good."[1] Chicago's last game had been the previous January in San Francisco. They were playing in the NFC Championship game against the 49ers. The winner would go onto the Super Bowl, but that wouldn't be Chicago. The 49ers beat the Bears badly, 23–0. It was a sad way to end the season.

So in 1985, the players and coaches agreed that their goal was to win the Super Bowl, nothing less. "I don't know about you guys," Ditka told the team just before the start of the season, "but second best isn't good enough for me."[2]

The Bears tore up the NFL in 1985 like hungry animals, winning their first twelve games of the season. Almost all of the wins were total blowouts and Chicago finished the 1985 season with a league-best 15–1 record.

Still, the Bears had to win all their playoff games. That wasn't a problem: They beat the New York Giants, 21–0, in the divisional round. In the NFC championship– the same game the Bears lost one year earlier– they slammed the Los Angeles Rams, 24–0.

Onward to the Big Game.

Shuffle Time

Two weeks separated the conference championships and the Super Bowl in New Orleans, so the Bears (and their opponents, the New England Patriots) had plenty of time to get ready. For Chicago, winning the Super Bowl simply felt like destiny. The Bears believed it so strongly that they put it to music in a rap song called the "Super Bowl Shuffle," which would be

The Chicago Bears Football Team

*B*ears fullback William "The Refrigerator" Perry spikes the ball after rushing for a touchdown in Super Bowl XX.

broadcast at halftime. Ten Bears rapped solos in the song, including Payton, McMahon, Perry, and linebackers Richard Dent and Mike Singletary.

On January 26, 1986, President Ronald Reagan opened Super Bowl XX by declaring, "May the best team win!"[3] With their record, the Bears were the best team. But just moments into the game, it didn't look like they were going to win. On the second play, quarterback McMahon made a handoff to Payton, who fumbled the football. (Later, McMahon insisted the fumble was his own fault because he called the wrong play.) The Patriots got the ball on Chicago's 19-yard line, and Tony Franklin kicked a field goal. One minute, nineteen seconds into the game, the Bears were losing, 3–0.

That slipped-up handoff would be the only time Chicago was behind. Kevin Butler kicked two first-quarter field goals of his own, sending Chicago ahead, 6–3. A couple of touchdowns followed, then another field goal. By halftime, the Bears were ahead 23–3. They doubled their points in the second half, winning the Super Bowl with a 46–10 victory. Quarterback McMahon scored twice on one-yard sneaks. At fullback, three-hundred pound Refrigerator Perry rumbled into the end zone for a score. The defense caused six turnovers and even had a safety.

Steve McMichael (left) and William Perry (right) carry Head Coach Mike Ditka off the field after the Chicago Bears defeated the New England Patriots 46–10 in Super Bowl XX.

The Chicago Bears Football Team

The Greatest

The only bad thing about the Bears' victory was that their best player, Payton, didn't score. "He's the greatest," said center Jay Hilgenberg. "He doesn't need a Super Bowl touchdown to be the greatest."[4]

In that year, the Chicago Bears were the greatest. The last time they had won an NFL championship was 1963. Twenty-three years was a long time to wait. "It was a long wait, but it was worth it," said Ditka, who had played on that 1963 team. "A lot of dreams have been fulfilled, a lot of frustrations have been ended."[5]

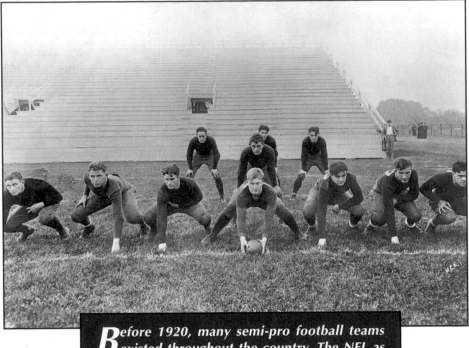

Before 1920, many semi-pro football teams existed throughout the country. The NFL as we know it today was not formed until 1922.

2

FROM CORN STARCH TO SUPER BOWLS

The Chicago Bears were made from corn starch. Really. The history of the Bears dates back to 1920 and a town called Decatur. Located about 170 miles from Chicago, Decatur was home to Staley Starch Works. The owner, A. E. Staley, was a big sports fan. His company sponsored a baseball team for the workers. The men would play and their families would watch.

Around this time, college football was popular. At Staley's request, plant superintendent George Chamberlain organized a football team in 1919. This Staley group was really good, and they beat a team from the nearby town of Arcola, 41–0.

Embarrassed, the Arcolans put together a team of college stars and tried to get the Staleys to play another game. Staley wouldn't let his team play. Instead, he decided to build his own superstar team. Someone suggested that he call 25-year-old George Halas, who had been an outstanding football and baseball player for the University of Illinois. Halas happily accepted the job of working in the starch plant, playing on the baseball team and building the football team. "I still had this football idea fixed in the back of my mind," Halas said many years later. "I wanted to give it a whirl, some way, sometime."[1]

In the spring of 1920, Staley also hired Ed "Dutch" Sternaman, the man who had recommended Halas.

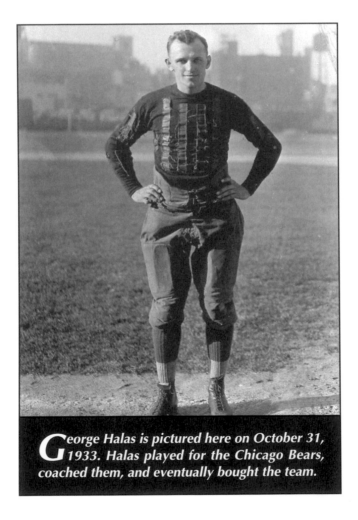

George Halas is pictured here on October 31, 1933. Halas played for the Chicago Bears, coached them, and eventually bought the team.

Together, Halas and Sternaman began signing up players. Halas was also looking for teams to play. Many teams existed, but it was difficult to figure out a game schedule. Halas thought the various teams should organize themselves into a league, and he said so in a letter to Canton Bulldogs manager Ralph Hay.

Joining A League

The idea of forming a league made sense to Hay. On September 17, 1920, he hosted a meeting inside the showroom of his automobile dealership in Canton, Ohio. Representatives of eleven teams (including Halas for the Staleys) sat on car fenders, figuring out how to run the new league. After two hours, they had agreed on the rules and decided to call the new league the American Professional Football Association (APFA).

The first season began that autumn, and the Staleys were good. With future Hall of Famers like end Guy Chamberlin, center George Trafton and halfback Jimmy Conzelman, Decatur finished with 10 wins, 1 tie and 2 losses.

After that first season, Staley made a difficult decision. An economic recession was affecting businesses across the United States, and his was no different. He could no longer could afford to fund the football team. Staley called Halas into his office and delivered the news, along with a generous offer. "Why don't you move the boys up to Chicago?" Staley said. "I think pro football can go over in a big way there. I'll give you $5,000 to help you get started. All I ask is that you continue to call the team the Staleys for one season."[2]

Halas quickly accepted. Who wouldn't be thrilled to be given a pro football team for free? Halas was also a little nervous: He would be the owner, general manager, coach and a player. That was a lot of responsibility, especially in a big city like Chicago.

Chicago Champs

In 1921, playing in Chicago's Wrigley Field, the Staleys won the APFA championship with a 9–1–1 record. After that season, the APFA changed its name

Football legend Red Grange, also known as the Galloping Ghost, played for the Bears in 1925, and then again from 1929 to 1934.

The Chicago Bears Football Team

to the National Football League. Halas was also thinking about new nicknames for his club around this time. He thought about calling the team the Cubs, just like the Chicago baseball team that also played in Wrigley Field. But when Halas thought about it further, he realized something. "Football players are much bigger than baseball players," he wrote in his autobiography, "so if baseball players are cubs, then football players must be bears!"[3]

It would take a few years before the Chicago Bears became famous. When the Bears were touring the nation in 1925, Halas and his star player, Red Grange, met President Calvin Coolidge at the White House. An Illinois senator introduced the player as "Red Grange, who plays with the Chicago Bears."

President Coolidge shook Grange's hand. "Nice to meet you, young man," he said. "I've always liked animal acts."[4]

*B*ears running back Walter Payton breaks through the New England Patriots defense in Super Bowl XX. Payton would end his career as the NFL's all-time leading rusher.

GREAT BEARS

Visitors to the Pro Football Hall of Fame in Canton, Ohio find that one out of every eight members is a Chicago Bear. That's more than any other team.

Since 1920, over 1,100 athletes have played for the Bears. So many have been memorable: One was Jim McMahon, whose rock-star sunglasses and outrageous comments created a character football fans will never forget. Another was Brian Piccolo, a young running back who played four years with the Bears before being diagnosed with cancer. His spirited struggle against the disease made him a hero even before his death in 1970, at age 26.

From McMahon to Piccolo, and for football greats like Red Grange and Walter Payton, Chicago has been a playing field for legends.

Red Grange

Many sports fans thought football was barbaric until they heard about the smooth-running Red Grange, who was a star at the University of Illinois in the early 1920s. As soon as Grange finished his college career, in 1925, Halas signed him to tour the United States with the Bears. The Galloping Ghost sometimes drew crowds of more than seventy thousand people. In those days, a crowd of just a few thousand was typical for football.

Opposing teams didn't want Grange to entertain those crowds, so they tried to keep the ball away from him. "Punting to Grange is like grooving one to Babe Ruth," said Paddy Driscoll, punter for the Bears' cross-town rivals, the Chicago Cardinals.[1]

Sid Luckman

When he graduated from Columbia University in 1939, Sid Luckman was planning to join his brothers in a trucking business. But Halas wanted Luckman so much that he traveled to New York and worked out a deal sitting at the quarterback's kitchen table.

Luckman was picked to run the Bears' new T formation, which was full of trickery like handoffs and faked passes. Things that quarterbacks do regularly today weren't so simple in 1940. "Every day I would spend hours in my room spinning and pivoting and practice handling the ball," Luckman said.[2]

Dick Butkus

During warm-ups, Dick Butkus would stare at the opposing team. If a player was smiling, Butkus would

18

pretend the guy was laughing at him. He'd get ready to strike like a poisonous rattlesnake. Even in practice, he tackled his teammates hard, but always cleanly.

The Bears' runners were thrilled to have Butkus on their side. Of course, no sensible person would want to play against him. "If I had a choice," said running back MacArthur Lane of the Green Bay Packers, "I'd sooner go one-on-one with a grizzly bear. I pray I can get up every time Butkus hits me."[3]

Gale Sayers

When stargazers see comets, the brilliant trails of light may last only a few seconds, then disappear. The Kansas Comet played the same way.

Dick Butkus holds up his jersey during a special ceremony to retire his number during halftime of a game in 1994.

*C*hicago Bears owner-coach George Halas goes over some plays with members of the team on August 4, 1947. Halas coached the Bears to 318 regular season victories.

4

PAPA BEAR

The story of George Halas in football actually begins on a baseball field. On a March afternoon in 1919, Halas was auditioning in Florida spring training for an outfielder job with the New York Yankees. In an exhibition game against the Brooklyn Dodgers, Halas was at the plate, facing Dodgers ace Rube Marquard.

Halas expected a fastball. It came, and he swatted the ball directly between the center and left fielder. As the outfielders ran to the fence, Halas whirled around the bases on his speedy feet.

First base . . . second . . . the throw was coming . . . a hook slide into third, and . . . SAFE!

A triple! Usually such a hit helps a young player make the club. But for Halas, it did the opposite. "That slide," he said, "was the beginning and the end of my baseball career."[1] Halas had injured his hip on the play. Though he played the 1919 season in the minor leagues, he lost his speed and retired.

On To Football

Baseball's loss was football's gain. He organized the Staleys team, helped set up the NFL, and moved the franchise to Chicago. In Chicago, Halas played for the Bears, coached them, and ran the front office. After the 1929 season, Halas retired as a player and coach and concentrated on his front-office duties.

By 1932, co-owner Sternaman wanted out of the Chicago Bears. He and Halas often disagreed on how to run the team, and Sternaman wanted to invest his money in other businesses. For $38,000, Halas could buy out Sternaman, and the Bears would belong to him alone. An agreement was reached: Halas had to come up with the $38,000 by August 9, 1933. If he did not, the Bears would belong completely to Sternaman.

To get the money, Halas borrowed from banks, his friends, his players, even his mother. When August 9 arrived, however, he still needed $5,000. "I was desperate," he said.[2] Luckily, an Illinois banker named C. K. Anderson called Halas with the $5,000 loan about thirty minutes before the money was due.

Saving his ownership of the team by minutes, Halas was now the man in charge. Able to do whatever he wanted, he put himself back in the head coach's job in 1933. For forty years Halas coached the Bears, though he took himself out of the head coach's job three more times. One of those times, he joined the Navy (1942-45) during World War II.

Virginia McCaskey, daughter of Chicago Bears team founder George Halas, owns the team today with her husband, Ed McCaskey.

Halas was a stickler for rules and was quick to fine any player who broke them. Things like training camp, daily practices, regular team meetings, and pregame curfews are normal for teams today. Halas is largely responsible for these practices becoming standard in the NFL.

The Family Business

In 1968, George Halas retired as a coach for the final time. The 1970s were rough decade for the Bears, who kept losing year after year. In 1975, team president

George "Mugs" Halas, Jr. (the first George's son) hired a well-known football man named Jim Finks to help rebuild the club. Finks, now a Hall of Famer, did his job by getting players like Walter Payton, Mike Singletary, Richard Dent, and many more.

Mugs died in 1979 at age fifty-four. George Halas, Sr. died four years later at age eighty-eight, but the club was still in the family's hands. Halas's daughter and son-in-law, Virginia and Ed McCaskey, asked their son Michael to become club president. He ran the Bears until 1999, when the club was turned over to current president Ted Phillips.

Mike Ditka coached the Bears from 1982 to 1992. He then went on to coach the New Orleans Saints fron 1997 to 2000.

The Chicago Bears Football Team

Iron Mike

During the 1960s, Coach Halas had on his team a fiery young tight end named Mike Ditka. Even as a young player, Ditka was the kind of guy who'd say anything to anybody. If he felt a veteran was being lazy in practice, he'd say so. His words were as strong as his skills: Ditka was a star player and the first tight end to be elected to the Pro Football Hall of Fame.

In the late 1970s, Ditka decided he wanted the Bears's head coaching job someday and wrote a letter to Halas expressing his interest. Hiring Ditka in 1982 was perhaps the last great move Halas made. Ditka had a bearlike personality, which Chicago needed. At times he could be calm and quiet, but usually he was roaring. Ditka's No. 1 goal, no matter what he was doing, was to win. "I hate to lose," Ditka said. "When I was a kid playing Little League baseball, boy I hated to lose. I cried. It just hurt my feelings to lose."[3]

Ditka did little losing for the Bears. In eleven seasons as coach, he won one Super Bowl (1986) and achieved a record of 112–68–0. Ditka departed after a disappointing 1992 season, but he'll forever be a Bear.

*B*ears fullback Bronko Nagurski is pictured here in 1943. The Bronk was a star player for the team in the 1930s, then returned for one season in 1943.

BEARS DYNASTY

There is none of them compare with our Chicago Bears.[1]

That line comes from the Bears' first fight song. It was written in 1922, one year after Chicago won its first football championship. Between 1920 and 1963, the Bears won eight league titles.

Chicago's fight song was rewritten in 1941 by Jerry Downs and was called "Bear Down, Chicago Bears." One of the lines goes, "Bear down, Chicago Bears, and let them know why you're wearing the crown."[2]

"The Bronk"

Why have the Chicago Bears worn so many crowns? Simple—they've had the stars. Chicago's back-to-back NFL champion teams of 1932 and 1933 were stocked with early superstars: Grange, fullback/kicker Jack Manders, and fullback Bronko Nagurski.

Nagurski was a human bulldozer. Defenders would rather tackle a locomotive. According to one story, Nagurski once ran out of bounds and crashed into a policeman on a horse, grounding the animal. In another story, Nagurski missed a tackle and ran out of bounds, knocking into a car and tearing off the fender. "When you hit him," Grange said, "it was like getting an electric shock. If you hit him above the ankles, you were likely to get yourself killed."[3]

Nagurski and Grange were key members of the Bears teams that won championships by beating the Portsmouth Spartans (9–0) in 1932 and the New York Giants (23–21) in 1933. Grange, in fact, made a great defensive play at the end of the 1933 Giants game to prevent a New York touchdown and save Chicago's two-point victory.

T-Formation Championships

Such heroic defensive players weren't needed in Chicago's next championship victory, which came in 1940. The Bears, playing the Redskins, were angry. Earlier in the year, after Washington beat Chicago, 7–3, the Bears complained about a referee's call. Redskins coach George Marshall called them "quitters" and "crybabies." The Bears wanted revenge and were eager for that championship game. Before the game, Marshall sent Halas a telegram that read: "Congratulations, you got me into this thing and I hope I have the pleasure of beating your ears off next Sunday."[4]

Marshall didn't get that pleasure. Fifty-five seconds into the game, the Bears scored a touchdown. From there, they were unstoppable: The final score, 73–0, remains the biggest blowout in NFL history. After the game, someone asked the Redskins' Sammy Baugh if the outcome would have been different had Washington's Charley Malone not dropped a first-quarter touchdown pass. Yes, Baugh replied. "The score would have been 73–6."[5]

The Bears Sid Luckman tackles Jimmy Johnstone (31) of the Washington Redskins during the NFL championship game on December 8, 1940.

Chicago won three more championships (1941, 1943, 1946) and became known as the best team of the 1940s. Using Halas's T formation, the Bears' leader was quarterback Sid Luckman. Luckman was also teamed with several future Hall of Famers: guard Danny Fortmann, halfback George McAfee, guard George Musso, tackle Joe Stydahar, and center Clyde "Bulldog" Turner.

The 1943 championship was special because it marked the short comeback of Bronko Nagurski. The Bronk had left football in 1937 and had become a successful professional wrestler. Now he was retired and living peacefully on a farm in Minnesota. Nagurski was offered $5,000 to return to the Bears and help them beat the Washington Redskins. With many athletes serving military duty overseas during World War II, there was a shortage of players. Nagurski agreed to return, and he helped Chicago defeat Washington, 41–21, for the title.

The '63 Defense

During the 1950s, the Bears were only an average team. Glory days returned in 1963, when a legendary defense led by coordinator George Allen pushed Chicago to an 11–1–2 record. Entering the championship game against the New York Giants, Chicago was a ten-point underdog. Quarterback Bill Wade scored two touchdowns, both of which came after the Bears' defense intercepted passes to put their offense in good scoring position. Those two scores were all the Bears needed to beat New York, 14–10 and

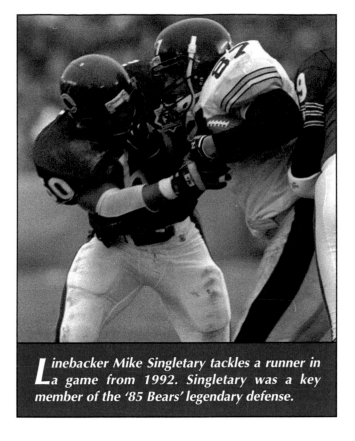

Linebacker Mike Singletary tackles a runner in a game from 1992. Singletary was a key member of the '85 Bears' legendary defense.

capture Chicago's first football crown in seventeen years.

Twenty-two years after that, people would be comparing the 1963 defense to that of the 1985 Bears. The 1963 team had stars like pass rushing defensive end Doug Atkins and linebacker Bill George. The 1985 version was led by tackle Dan Hampton and linebacker Mike Singletary. "I think the defenses are quite similar," Allen said in 1985. "Both very physical. Both excellent at forcing turnovers. Both capable of winning the championship of defense if the offense doesn't make too many mistakes."[6]

One final similarity: Both Chicago clubs were champions.

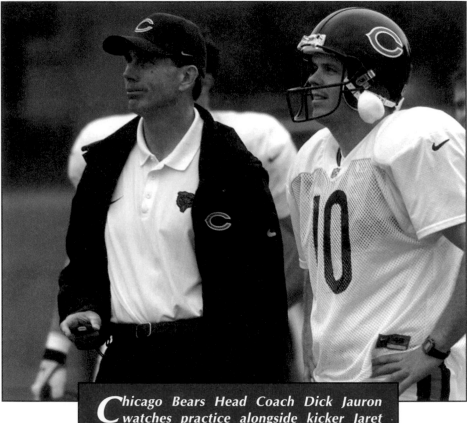

*C*hicago Bears Head Coach Dick Jauron watches practice alongside kicker Jaret Holmes during training camp in July of 2000.

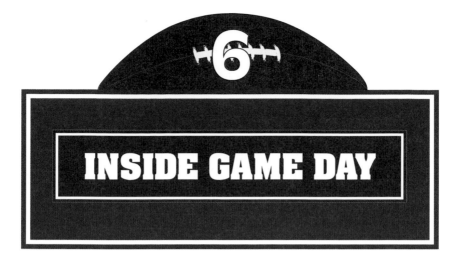

INSIDE GAME DAY

This is when championships are won, step by step. This is when things are at their quietest. This is game day— time for the Bears to wrap a week's worth of strategy, practice and study into a well-planned winning package.

Everything began last night, when players and coaches gathered in a hotel for a six o'clock team dinner and meeting. Even for Sunday home games, players will stay in a downtown Chicago hotel Saturday evening. That way, they're assured of a proper meal and a peaceful night's sleep. Players have a few hours free before an 11:00 P.M. curfew. Assistant coaches go room to room, conducting a bed check, making sure the lights are out.

A Focused Morning

Sunday morning, players carpool to Soldier Field. They must arrive two hours before kickoff. Normally, that means everyone is in the locker room by 10:00 A.M. Walk into the Bears' locker room two hours before game time and you'll hear little talking or noise. Some players will be lying on the floor, eyes closed, envisioning themselves making great plays in a couple hours. Others will be seated on their locker stools, listening to headphones or reading the newspaper.

Everyone except the kicker and punter will be getting their ankles taped by the athletic trainers. (A massive amount of tape is used. By year's end, the average NFL training staff will use almost seventy-one miles of tape.) The trainers are also fixing any ailments, like if someone has a stomachache, and helping players put on knee braces.

The equipment staff, meanwhile, has neatly laid out all the uniforms. They're now troubleshooting any equipment problems and helping guys get dressed. "Football uniforms aren't always the easiest to get on, especially when you're talking about the running backs and receivers," says Scott Hagel of the Bears' public relations department. "Their jerseys are on so tight so that guys can't just grab hold of their jerseys to tackle them."[1]

In the upper portions of the stadium, the Bears' video crew is readying cameras and film. They tape the whole game from a sideline and end-zone view. On Monday, the coaches will use this tape to review the game and analyze what went right or wrong on each play. During the game, the video crew also operates an instant camera which takes pictures of

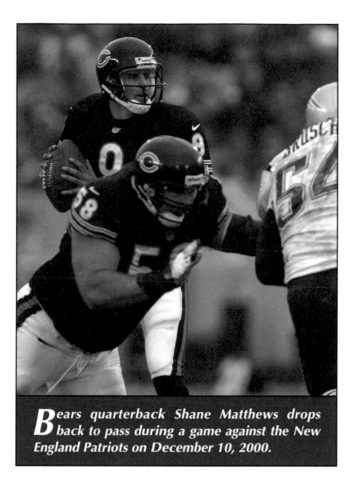

Bears quarterback Shane Matthews drops back to pass during a game against the New England Patriots on December 10, 2000.

formations being used by the other team. These are given to the Bears coaches, who may adjust their strategy based on what they see in the pictures.

Between one hundred and two hundred writers, broadcasters, and scouts are gathering in the press box. Throughout the game they will be provided with play-by-play statistics, while several televisions provide instant replays.

The Aftermath

Within ten minutes after the game, all the reporters converge on the locker room area. Many will attend

Head Coach Dick Jauron's press conference. Others will go directly into the locker room to interview Bears players. After they shower, dress, and give interviews, the players may leave. The training staff sticks around to take care of any injuries, while the equipment staff has several loads of laundry to do. Writers will be at Soldier Field for two or three more hours, finishing their stories and filing them for Monday's newspaper.

While all this is happening, a Bears worker named Rick Spielman has been watching a game in another city. As Chicago's director of pro scouting, Spielman is an advance man, who watches whatever team the

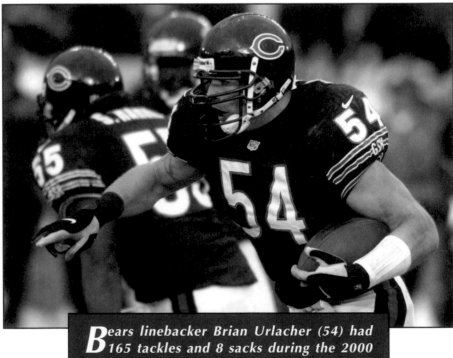

Bears linebacker Brian Urlacher (54) had 165 tackles and 8 sacks during the 2000 season and was recognized as the NFL Defensive Rookie of the Year.

Bears will be playing the following week, then writes a detailed report for Coach Jauron and his staff. Spielman's report is delivered Monday morning, so the coaches can use it immediately. For the Chicago Bears to keep their winning ways, they must always be ready for the next challenge.

STATISTICS

Team Record

The Bears History

YEARS	LOCATION	W	L	T	PCT.	PLAYOFFS	NFL CHAMPS
1920	Decatur	10	1	2	.909	—	—
1921–29	Chicago	74	30	17	.712	—	1921 (APFA Champs)
1930–39	Chicago	85	28	11	.752	1–0	1932, 1933
1940–49	Chicago	81	26	3	.757	5–1	1940, 1941, 1943, 1946
1950–59	Chicago	70	48	2	.593	0–2	None
1960–69	Chicago	67	65	6	.508	1–0	1963
1970–79	Chicago	60	83	1	.420	0–2	None
1980–89	Chicago	92	60	0	.605	5–4	1985
1990–99	Chicago	73	87	0	.456	2–3	None

The Bears Today

YEAR	W	L	PCT.	COACH	DIVISION FINISH
1990	11	5	.688	Mike Ditka	1st
1991	11	5	.688	Mike Ditka	2nd
1992	5	11	.313	Mike Ditka	4th
1993	7	9	.438	Dave Wannstedt	4th
1994	9	7	.563	Dave Wannstedt	4th
1995	9	7	.563	Dave Wannstedt	3rd
1996	7	9	.438	Dave Wannstedt	3rd
1997	4	12	.250	Dave Wannstedt	5th
1998	4	12	.250	Dave Wannstedt	5th
1999	6	10	.375	Dick Jauron	5th

W=Wins   L=Losses   T=Ties   PCT.=Percentage

Total History

SEASON RECORD				PLAYOFFS		
W	L	T	PCT.	W	L	NFL CHAMPIONSHIPS
612	428	42	.588	14	12	9

Coaching Records

COACH	YEARS COACHED	RECORD*	CHAMPIONSHIPS
George Halas	1920–29, 1933–42, 1946–55, 1958–67	318–148–31	APFA Champions 1921, NFL Champions 1932, 1933, 1940, 1941, 1946, 1963
Ralph Jones	1930–32	24–10–7	–
Heartly (Hunk) Anderson Luke Johnsos**	1942–45	23–11–2	NFL Champions 1943
John "Paddy" Driscoll	1956–57	14–9–1	None
Jim Dooley	1968–71	26–36–0	None
Abe Gibron	1972–74	11–30–1	None
Jack Pardee	1975–77	20–22–0	None
Neill Armstrong	1978–81	30–34–0	None
Mike Ditka	1982–92	106–62–0	Super Bowl Champions, 1985
Dave Wannstedt	1993–98	40–56–0	None

*Includes regular-season games only
**Co-coaches during War years

Great Bears Career Statistics

PASSING							
PLAYER	SEASONS	Y	G	ATT	COMP	YDS	TD
George Blanda	1949–58	26	340	4,007	1,911	26,920	236
Sid Luckman	1939–50	12	128	1,744	904	14,686	137

Great Bears Career Statistics (continued)

RUSHING

PLAYER	SEASONS	Y	G	ATT	YDS	AVG	TD
Red Grange	1925, 1929–34	9	96	170*	569*	3.3*	21*
Bronko Nagurski	1930–37, 1943	9	97	633	2,778	4.4	25
Walter Payton	1975–87	13	190	3,838	16,726	4.4	110
Gale Sayers	1965–71	7	68	991	4,956	5.0	39

KICKING

PLAYER	SEASONS	Y	POINTS	EXTRA POINTS	FIELD GOALS
Kevin Butler	1985–95	13	1,208	413	265

DEFENSE

PLAYER	SEASONS	Y	G	TACK	AST	TOT	SACK	INT	FUM
Dick Butkus	1965–73	9	120	*	*	*	*	22	25
Richard Dent	1983–93, 1995	15	170	*	*	*	137.5	8	13
Mike Singletary	1981–92	12	179	1,488**	*	*	19	7	12

OFFENSIVE/DEFENSIVE LINEMEN

PLAYER	SEASONS	Y	G	ACCOMPLISHMENTS
Danny Fortmann	1936–43	8	86	All-NFL 1937–43.
Clyde "Bulldog" Turner	1940–52	13	138	Eight INTs led league in 1942. In 1947, returned an interception 96 yards for a TD.

*Official records not maintained or are incomplete
**Unofficial statistic

CHAPTER NOTES

Chapter 1. A Super Win

1. *Chicago Tribune*, "Bears to End Vacation at Camp," July 21, 1985, <http://www.chicagotribune.com> (January 30, 2001).

2. Richard Whittingham, *The Bears: A 75-Year Celebration* (Dallas: Taylor Publishing, 1994), p. 181.

3. Dave Anderson, "The Best Team," *The New York Times*, January 27, 1986, p. C1.

4. George Vecsey, "Payton Misses Out on Scoring Parade," *The New York Times*, January 27, 1986, p. C10.

5. Gary Pomerantz, "Bears Don't Shuffle, They Waltz, 46–10," *Washington Post*, January 27, 1986, p. C1.

Chapter 2. From Corn Starch to Super Bowls

1. Howard Roberts, *The Chicago Bears* (New York: G. P. Putnam's Sons, 1947), p. 7.

2. George Vass, *George Halas and the Chicago Bears* (Chicago: Henry Regnery Co., 1971), p. 36.

3. Chicago Bears, *1999 Chicago Bears Media Guide* (Chicago: Chicago Bears Public Relations Department, 1999), p. 4.

4. John M. Carroll, *Red Grange and the Rise of Modern Football* (Urbana/Chicago: University of Illinois Press, 1999), p. 114.

Chapter 3. Great Bears

1. George Vass, *George Halas and the Chicago Bears* (Chicago: Henry Regnery Co., 1971), p. 77.

2. Ibid., p. 125.

3. "Chicago Bears–Hall of Fame Dick Butkus," n.d., <http://www.chicagobears.com/bearsalley/dickbutkus.cfm> (January 30, 2001).

4. M.B. Roberts, "Fame Couldn't Wait for Sayers," n.d., <http://www.espn.go.com/sportscentury/features/00016460.html> (January 30, 2001).

5. H & S Media Staff, *Sweetness: The Courage and Heart of Walter Payton* (Chicago, Ill.: Triumph Books, 1999), p. 45.

6. "Chicago Bears–Hall of Fame Mike Singletary," n.d., <http://www.chicagobears.com/bearsalley/mikesingletary.cfm> (January 30, 2001).

Chapter 4. Papa Bear

1. George Vass, *George Halas and the Chicago Bears* (Chicago: Henry Regnery Co., 1971), p. 6.

2. Richard Whittingham, *The Bears: A 75-Year Celebration* (Dallas: Taylor Publishing, 1994), p. 34.

3. Don Pierson, "The Coach Who Hates to Lose," *Chicago Tribune*, November 17, 1985, p. 1

Chapter 5. Bears Dynasty

1. Richard Whittingham, *The Bears: A 75-Year Celebration* (Dallas: Taylor Publishing, 1994), p. 87.

2. Chicago Bears, *1999 Chicago Bears Media Guide* (Chicago: Chicago Bears Public Relations Department, 1999), p. 5.

3. Vic Carucci, contributor, *75 Seasons: The Complete Story of the National Football League, 1920–1995* (Atlanta: Turner Publishing, Inc., 1994), p. 44.

4. Whittingham, p. 125.

5. Ibid.

6. Cooper Rollow, "How Does Bear Defense Stack Against '63 Team? Ask Allen," *Chicago Tribune*, November 10, 1985, p. 15.

Chapter 6. Inside Game Day

1. Author interview with Scott Hagel, April 2000.

GLOSSARY

AFC—The American Football Conference.

APFA—The American Professional Football Association, founded in 1920, was the first professional football league. The APFA changed its name to the National Football League (NFL) in 1922.

free agency—An agreement between the players' association and the owners that allows players to sign with other teams when their contracts have expired.

Heisman Trophy—An award given to the best college player of the year.

linebackers—The players who line up behind the defensive linemen. They are responsible for stopping running backs who have gone past the defensive linemen and for covering running backs and tight ends when they go out for passes.

Most Valuable Player (MVP)—The player who is voted the most valuable in a league.

NFC—The National Football Conference.

NFL—The National Football League. Since 1970, the NFL has been made up of the teams in the AFC and the NFC.

playoff games—Games played between the division winners and the wild-card teams at the end of the regular season to determine the world champions.

Pro Bowl—An All-Star game played after the Super Bowl. It is played by the top players from both the AFC and the NFC, who play against each other to see which conference has the better players.

Pro Football Hall of Fame—A museum in Canton, Ohio, where the greatest football players are showcased.

quarter—One of four fifteen-minute periods in a football game.

Super Bowl—The NFL Championship Game played between the winners of the AFC and the NFC.

"Super Bowl Shuffle"—A rap video made by the 1985 Chicago Bears prior to winning Super Bowl XX.

T-formation—When the fullback lines up directly behind the quarterback. Beside the fullback are the left and right halfbacks.

FURTHER READING

Chicago Bears Staff. *Chicago Bears.* White Plains, N.Y.: Everett Sports Publishing & Marketing, 1998.

H & S Media Staff. *Sweetness: The Courage and Heart of Walter Payton.* Chicago, Ill.: Triumph Books, 1999.

Italia, Bob. *The Chicago Bears.* Edina, Minn.: Abdo & Daughters, 1996.

Koslow, Philip. *Walter Payton.* Broomall, Pa.: Chelsea House Publishers, 1994.

Lace, William W. *Top 10 Football Rushers.* Hillside, N.J.: Enslow Publishers, Inc., 1994.

Mausser, Wayne. *Chicago Bears Facts & Trivia,* 2nd ed. Neshkoro, Wis.: E. B. Houchin Company, 1995.

McDonough, Will. *75 Seasons: The Complete Story of the National Football League, 1920–1995.* Atlanta, Ga.: Turner Publishing, Inc., 1994.

Savage, Jeff. *Top 10 Professional Football Coaches.* Springfield, N.J.: Enslow Publishers, Inc., 1998.

Whittingham, Richard et. al. *The Bears: A 75-Year Celebration.* Dallas, Tex.: Taylor Publishing, 1994.

Wulffson, Don L. *When Human Heads Were Footballs.* New York: Aladdin Paperbacks, 1998.

INDEX

WHERE TO WRITE AND INTERNET SITES

http://www.chicagobears.com

http://sports.nfl.com/2000/newsnotes?team=3

http://football.espn.go.com/nfl/index

Chicago Bears
Halas Hall
1000 Football Drive
Lake Forest, IL 60045